salmonpoetry

Diverse Voices from Ireland and the World

the arts council
an chomhairle
ealaíon

funding
literature
artscouncil.ie

Jamais Vu

Poems by
PAUL PERRY

Published in 2022 by
Salmon Poetry
Cliffs of Moher, County Clare, Ireland
Website: www.salmonpoetry.com
Email: info@salmonpoetry.com

ISBN 978-1-915022-18-9

Cover & Title Page Image:
Cover image "Nouvelle Lune," acrylic, marble powder, and pure pigment on canvas,
by Eric Roux-Fontaine, with the artist's kind permission.

Cover Design & Typesetting: *Siobhán Hutson*

Printed in Ireland by Sprint Print

*Salmon Poetry gratefully acknowledges the support of
The Arts Council / An Chomhairle Ealaíon*

for my parents Frank and Eithne

Contents

jamais vu

noun

ja·mais vu | \ ˌzhȧ-ˌme-ˈv̄ie , ˌjä-ˌmā-ˈvü \

: from the French meaning "never seen"

: a disorder of memory characterized by the illusion that the familiar is being encountered for the first time

: often described as the opposite of *déjà vu*, jamais vu involves a sense of eeriness and the observer's impression of seeing the situation for the first time, despite rationally knowing that they have been in the situation before

Puffins in Marley Park

Stay together. Know what to do. Where to be. And what to say. Or not to say. They.

Silent at sea.

Like a vision and not at all where they should be.

On boulder scree, and sea stacks—

anointing my pelagic soul with the natty tiny chainsaws they have. As voice.

Or calling out from a cliff face on the western coast, or north.

No sand eel or sprat for you here, before you turn tail, and the sun rises over Three Rock.

My feet follow the shadow of

I do what I do—
stepping again counter-clockwise around the instruments of my life.

Jesus of no thought.

And the girl who came to see the puffins on the island all those years ago?

Where?
What name?
Did you?
Or go with—the ghosts

of the halfway house.

The songs of survival.

Our bones colliding against the memory of our first home and the green stone I etched our initials onto before placing it into the wet cement.

Each note of Pergolesi's Stabat Mater traced by my finger and held and guided by yours like the birds the girl travelled across the world to see, like the wind without, or a puffin sky-fishing.

Or like the divers diving for the fresh raw heart of morning.

The first. And the last.

Shepherd's Purse

In the field — shepherd's purse: to be seen even in the dark.

Think on it — after the gravel paths, after the roads — uneven and achingly long, across the cold promise the border makes to a sloping field, to a ditch.

A ditch like any other. A ditch I have known — since.

Imagine them: green, slender, from crown to root, a rosette of radical leaves, smooth, arrow-shaped and above them numerous small, white, inconspicuous flowers.

There was no need to ask the man to kneel but he did, as if he were going to beg forgiveness, which he did not, nor did he ask for his life.

He named his children and his wife, murmured to his own private God.

Overhead, there was the sound of pine shifting, the moon winnowing in the distance.

So, nothing terrible about the night then, if you do not count the earth tilting, or the sound in the undergrowth of a passage from this world to the next.

More than that I remember the flat-seed pouch:
weed some call it, as if to flourish and seed in the poorest soil is to be just that.

They are everywhere now — it seems to me, populating my field of vision like a generative disease, an affliction.

Look: a man walks into a field. A field with shepherd's purse.

He falls.
He falls again.
Every day, from this day until kingdom come, he falls into the embrace of a field of flowers, into shepherd's purse.

To a Ghost

We sit in the room. We talk. It is my life you describe.
You say it is your own. Tell me again how it was.

The rain is lashing. Your handwriting uneven.

The other details you maintain are unimportant.

Talk about the moonlight then. In your childhood. It was thin as blood.

It was never there.

So sleep—whose kiss is this on your hot forehead?
Whose kiss?
So sleep –

There is a noise from downstairs. Imagine your mother baking.
It is not her. Or your father singing.

It is not him.

Downstairs, while you sleep or try to sleep, is something else.

It matters what you call it.

It matters that you can. So speak to me again of your life.
It is mine as well.

Not the wind, not the flag

i.m. Pat O'Brien

I rode all morning
towards the sun
up Cruagh to the Featherbeds
past Kippure, over the Gap
towards Laragh
so little traffic,
the heather turning purple
in the autumn light,
the hill before me
like a rough beast,
somewhere in the distance
is Lough Dan
below me Lough Tey,
it's wild to have the wind
rush through me like this
as if I am a parchment
too full of illegible script
and each pedal stroke
each breath erases
all the garbled speech
and word-horde
from my body
washes it out clean
and clean out
down then fast towards Djouce,
Luggala to the East
a waterfall smoking heavenward
fantastical route, divine transport
this then is where I am
away from the city
weaving my way
through the ancient woods
where the mystic waters flow
keep on the wind cries
go deep the stones call out

even as the light changes
and the sky darkens
even as the clouds converge
and the rain threatens
the soul remains
unrepentant
keep on, it cries
and the blood from my heart
pulses through my body
ever strongly
even as time passes
ever so and when the road dips
and you find yourself on a pathway
leading somewhere
you have never been
do not be afraid
go there friend
for the road will lead you
where you need to go
and your guide will be
all the forgotten words
of childhood
all the poems and promises
of adolescence
all the letters torn together
in parting
watch them scattering in the wind
like confetti
like dust
watch them float away
like the breath which leaves me now
and which carries your name
don't doubt it
branch and root
down to the last syllable
of your being

Birdsong, the moon

The rain the dark the coming night yes and the garden of the clock grown wild.

Yes the moon birdsong hardly. Let me keep my sorrow pure. Yes I did a mirage you didn't understand.

No for shadow you loped around and tried to kill your shadow yes my dew had disappeared with the sun yes. You asked for meaning no I said I was empty and impermanent.

I want to meet your father no you can't he's dead you will be my father. No I do not exist there is nothing to lose nothing to lose I do not exist no.

You will be my father yes he's dead you can't no I want to meet your father.

I was empty and impermanent I said no you asked for meaning yes. My dew disappeared with the sun yes try to kill your shadow. Lope around no for shadow you didn't understand.

I did a mirage yes keep my sorrow pure let me.

Hardly birdsong the moon yes and the garden of the clock. Grown wild yes the coming night the dark the rain.

Wallace Stevens in Lahinch

The life of the sea is only that because he is he, because he walks into the village, and through the village.

Whether it is Easter or it is not and that the music from a church in Ennistymon is baroque may or may not be important, even in the wake of scandal, of one boy taking his sister's life.

If all this is happening, and it might or might not be, and it is and it isn't—consider the question: whose footsteps are you walking in? It was Easter. The bars were closed, but the hotel was open for business.

The rehearsal was ongoing. The violins primed. The resin falling like an Easter snow.

The distance had been measured. We cannot discuss a fire. If there was a real one or not.

He was walking through your life like a ghost.

From one village to the next, you could almost hear the note—but whether it was the final note or not, that was something even the sound of his footfall could not tell you.

the ancient self

the children vacated the house quiet bar the echo of the alarms after the power cut pinging like a firecracker from one house to another and the aeroplane overhead and the children two down singing and calling out

bring on the night I say bring back the candles and creaks the huddle and safety of darkness a natural and indifferent flame to see the wavering but steadfast shadow step with guile and purpose from your only human body

Echoes of the One

Yesterday I felt empty
Not the kind of universal me
But nothing at all
All moods rise and fall
If the fatigue is not mine
It is not fatigue
Acceptance
To what aim for what purpose
But bills to pay
Why can I not still the mind
The sleeping seaminess
I went there too
To the burned forest
To the building sites
To a boy climbing a tree
Falling through its branches
Yesterday

There simply was no me
I sometimes feel
Void
Are empty and impotent
Then to whom does it belong
But resignation
There are only echoes of the one
Nothing to achieve
Amends to make
Daytime dead neon light
Waiting for night
Found my way back
To the shorn field
To the outskirts of the city
To another
Yesterday I felt empty
There simply was no me

Leonora's Violin

It is a tomato.
If you say so or a flamingo. Or a whatnot.

It is the laughter you gather at dusk.
It is the talk-talk guffaw and shush of the wind.

It is the rain in a glass jar. Ha or the sun pooling at your feet.
It is the sound of love.
It is love too.

My father as a child walks a donkey on Sandymount Strand

I took the donkey home. It was lame, and old. Herman was its name. Its owner, a German from Mainz. He had lived here since the war. A nice man who also played the concertina.

He baked his own bread. It tasted like a soul made of flour. He cut me a slice. Here, he said. Taste it. It comes all the way from Ober Olm where it has been resting in the earth.

The parcel it came in was also precious.

It was? I said.

Yes, the case of my concertina.

I bit into the bread, and the man began to sing.

The Double

It was in a bar, small and dark, cave-like in fact where, on the Keys, after all those years, I found him; he did not look surprised.

He smiled, actually—I remembered the smile. It had lost its infectiousness, but not its generous appeal.

His skin was tanned, his hand mottled. I recognised a slight tremor to the fingers.

The stool next to him stood vacant.

There was no sign of any other custom.

The barman breathed in the shadows.

Outside, winter nudged at the door. Its bright glare had made me squint, but still I noticed a cairn of ash at his feet.

Something on the jukebox skipped: Elvis gasping about a chapel.

He did not say *old friend*, not in words, but the way he dropped his head, almost imperceptibly, to the bar, to his hands, suggested as much.

Then the light from the portal-window caught his rheumy eye. His finger tapped the bar, his lips expelled all manner of unspoken rumour.

I glimpsed the faded green ink of a tattoo on the back of his neck: *homo fugue*. He turned to me.

Two glasses appeared.

The restless brush of a finger across the bridge of his nose—code for a life lived without change.

A shadow crossed the window and for a moment it was dark.

I can't tell if he said sit, but the word sprouted in my mind.

And I knew then that if I did—sit, that is—I would feel the fetid heat rise about me:

feel too the lurid burn of how my thirst might then be slaked, reach for and wear the same old stained cotton shirt he wore.

Exchange not pleasantries, but places, my pulse quickening in my blood, and forget for this lifetime at least every promise I had ever made.

Evidence

The mind's agile magic conjures the scene—the possibility of peace, an end to suffering.

Take the path by the lake, and walk about it—you did not know she was dying, but why else would she have gone back through the years like that, recalling with unaffected joy?

There was no self-pity to this woman, do you hear, how the factory work was work, how the dances on a Friday were fun, and that shows from London came to the Gaiety!

You took a phone call, excused yourself; it was the lawyer, calling about what he was calling about. You said what needed to be said and returned to the room.

When you stood there first, she said, I didn't know who it was, like you were a vision or something.

She was smiling. The TV in the corner was on mute. Other details? The mind stops short at (re)invention.

In this instance. For respect. For lack of evidence. Or whatnot. I stood. I sat. I stood again.

Not a vision, I said before I left. No, she said. Not a vision, after all.

Speaking Irish with my Daughter

The snow was falling.

We walked through the graveyard.

The candles lit: red icons in the night.

Jesu Christi in view, arís:

Window shopping for a soul.

My daughter—she is teaching me, telling me again how to say the words I once knew, but had forgotten, or never knew—subject, and verb:

I want.
I need.
I love.

Offering

I wanted the wrong things,
rushed and raved about the world for them
and none of it brought me anything but pain.

I did not pray nor was I grateful for what was simple.

Today, my daughter sings to the *spideog*,
the garden is overgrown, wasps swarm the azalea

and a flower called self-heal blossoms in the corner
where we sat last night without talking.

Voices carry on the breeze, the sound of a lawnmower,
and a church bell ringing.

I stop, ask for help; I am not beyond that—or writing
about grief and repair.

So much is waiting to be done:

the sun reveals itself from the cloud cover.

My body accepts the heat, and gratefully
not even the siren in the distance can trouble me now,

but I wanted you to know this:

that if there were some salve for your pain,
some solace I could lend,
I would offer it to you willingly, and with love.

Poem for an Unaccompanied Voice

we sat on the roof
chopping stray branches and laughed

that was a hundred years ago

afterwards

we played music at the fair
ate noodles sitting down

later again we painted
the porch
the wrong colour
some were
unhappy
not me

baking bread was another
good thing
from that time

across the yard
the sound of children's voices

the dust of
flour
on my hands
of years

Fragment

October and the rain is warm
the light moving across the water's surface

is there and not there like a voice you remember

say your mother's
youthful as once she was

on a day like this
embracing the sunshine breaking through

or watching it trace
between her fingertips so real

you can almost believe again in the silence
between you, her breath on your cheek

while you lay ill in bed
and in only a moment

a bell is ringing or your father
is singing in the kitchen about strangers

and without even an echo or the echo
of an echo all of this is gone and

we're walking again to the Hellfire Club
or the Sugar Loaf, it's Sunday

there's not much traffic and on the hills
as you run, twigs and small black pellets

are vanishing beneath your feet

The End of Summer

white chrysanthemums
a silent elegy
for summer

I will not have to tell you
when the future has arrived
you will know

sleeping alone
I heard the cuckoo
It was still dark

I cannot write what I want to write

a golden hare in the garden
looks up
and is gone

outside the window
the drip drip of the rain
onto the child's bicycle seat

I can't sleep I won't

cutting branches
from the overgrown elm
which stands between our wall
and theirs

two scooters lie
in the driveway
discarded

I pray for change
I pray for the end of summer

a siren in the distance
music on a radio
I try to leave the past behind

two missed phone calls
no call back
a stillness

the house silent
and expectant
waiting for the laughter
and the tears

putting my sandals away
and looking for socks
School starts tomorrow

Cycling with you on the crossbar
up the hill
you can do it, you can do it

You are only five
You were only five

Now I am cycling home alone
A pocket of blue
the trail of a plane

No bags packed
No passport at the ready
No calls to make

This is what I want to say to you:

I am staying
I was always staying
I am here
I am here
I am here

The Room with the Yellow Door

The belt
on
the floor
takes
me there
to
the room
with
the yellow
door

to its
stark
separateness, its
dank
fecundity. A
makeshift
bookshelf. A
stolen
desk covered
with
paper, and
half-written
poems. A
sliding
window I
snuck
my booze
through.
And a
stool
I stood
on
one night
unsure

reaching to
the
hook in
the
ceiling shining
my
belt knotted
my
neck taut
my
breath listless
in
the room
with
the yellow
door

which I
had
forgotten until
now
when I
saw
it again
in
the curve
of
the belt
on
the floor.

16

Found by the caretaker in the school corridor—
not early signs, but evidence of

a shadow self—

walked home alone in the early hours,
how long it took,

a teenager, a schoolboy:
what wretched thing had I tried to expel,

I still don't know—

but that it required a punishment, a purge.

My father sat at the kitchen table,
half asleep, a bottle by his side.

I woke him as I made my way inside—

by my actions I had only tried to show him
that he could be proud:

by his words he had only tried to warn me,
but of what I did not know.

Love is a Decision

I was determined not
to be tricked into

using words.

He hit me:
what do I feel?

I was about to say pain,
but said nothingness.

The days went on.
I avoided the others,
stopped laughing.

At times, it drove me crazy
rattling in my brain
not allowed to think

of anything else.

I jump up and throw it out.

Other times,
I go down.
Down.
Down with it,
down beneath words

where my breath is gentle.

It's like looking up
through a lake
and the surface is a sentence—

what it reads is nothingness.

What it says is love.

I am a crowd. I am a lonely man. I am nothing

I walk past the snow-covered apple orchard.

With its single black crow on a naked bough, the mountains look high.

What is it that I lack?
I want to go deeper, see clearer.

Today I planted flowers. I feel I have died in a way.
I rescued this notebook from a fire.

It's sunny. I'm watching the beans grow.

The clock stops. I stay up late.

I love to stand in the rain for the longest time without getting wet.

The bird in the apple blossoms
shook
the moisture from its feathers and sang.

I, in sympathy,
shook
in my raincoat and was silent.

Again, the sunflowers

A perpetual November of the soul
welcome and with it the white chrysanthemums
and the rain, which baptises the loneliest of days
with desire, and creates an anthem
for those years, or should it be an elegy?

Again the sunflowers,
the bicycles, a yellow telephone box,
it's my birthday, don't you know.
On the roof of the disused barn, a stork.
Rehearsals for a life
we are not going to live.

Tangermünde, the joy in just saying it,
lying by the Elbe, Silke was there,
I don't know why, we must have laughed and talked
and back in Wust there was dancing,
was that the first year or the one after?
One drink followed another, coffee, Kuchen,
remember Ingrid's, mole eyes—
they called me in the morning, and Uta's,
little Kneipe on the corner, the cobblestones too:
Icka me seife kaufen, neh, lieber wasche ich
mich nicht, Berliner Dialekt, jemand hat gesagt –
Ja, was weiss ich? And the tent on that first
night, erecting it, haphazardly in a storm,
was it a storm, yes, there was wind, and rain,
because we wanted to be together,
a forest around us, fires at night, and singing,
the first year, the first only, because within it
there was innocence, and can I say love?
You can, you may, then something changed.
The drawings I sent were black and ghostly
and composed under the influence,
and the confluence of demons, I can say that too,
now I can, all these years later, you will

allow me that, I was boy, and a boy knows nothing
and a shadow came to … can we talk of the shadow,
or is it too early, I do no write
what I am supposed to write, I do not …
there was talk and translation of the dirty
old town, and in the church, there were hymns—

What will you show me, what did you sing?
I can't remember, if you had a song,
You were quiet, grey eyes, blue eyes.
You were mystical, mythical,
spellbound, and abandoned, that was your
word—and you had your own language
too, was I your shadow, enough of that

There was a knock on the door.
Flowers—were these the irises,
painted onto the wall, strewn?
That was an indication, a sign
if ever there was one, if ever you needed
or looked for one. There was something
hidden or secret in language which would
give you the key, and the password,
the shibboleth, but when you did not,
could not find it, something else,
something which was not the yellow,
green blush, presenting itself, and with it
came the loss of control, of calm,
of the silence which you had carried around inside you.

Evenings when we walked home in the dusk,
your lips stinging, and your hair wet, neither
of us speaking, that was not a violation,
or presentiment or anything other
than what it was:

the dead speaking through us
willing us to listen,
to their testimony, to their warning:
Hoer zu, mein Kind.

There was a fortune teller, a man would you believe
who played the bass guitar with a show
band and with it he had a message—this was before the party
before the race, and the hitchhiking,
alone, it was another time, or you were lucky,
no, it was another time, because that was
how we all got home too,
remember the van with the chickens in the back,
jump in, or the Mercedes—rich woman ... la di da.
The fortune teller, there was more than one,
as if you couldn't bear the uncertainty of the future.
Or was it something else, most likely,
but I don't know what it was or is, because
it's buried somewhere in the sand,
and leave it there, will you, for the time being?

Lost your calmness, she said.
Once years later.
~~As if, as if, she had nothing to do with that.~~
Strike.
What point is there in trying to find ...
an image, or metaphor for the heart –
when it is a metaphor itself
for something far more complex,
inscrutable, a convoluted network, of
misremembered memories,
Of imaginings, of ... and so on.

Threw the Tarot away.
Scared.
Now let us not deny what a prayer
might be, because you have needed them.
Because nobody taught you to cope
~~With the volcano of~~ ...
~~Created~~ gentle, sensitive,
Hyper-so
To light and words,
To the sound of a person's voice—
And the generous, or censorious notes
Therein.

Back to Tangermünde.
There was a time I needed
nothing
but your voice to feel safe.
Your scent, was it almond, was it ...
a bridge—that was somewhere else,
but up these hills, at night, you can see the city,
Three Rock, the Poolbeg chimneys.
We were only kids,
with sleeping bags, and a story.
And don't forget this:
we knew how to laugh, if not how to dance.
And our talk was private, and real
and it sang out into the night
like a melody, like a lament,
which we as the last of our kind can make
and only make.

You see, there was that.
We were, you could say, if you had a mind to, something, after all.

A Child Being Taught to Walk

the trace of Rembrandt's hand
back and forth between mother and sister
when the sun is setting
her shirt ragged
a red coat if I remember correctly
there were keys in my hand
to entice you one step after another
your sing-song blue eyes
your mother playing the violin
the crucial aspects of the scene are transient
the alchemy of memory a mark,
a stroke, its relation, what it depicts
as transparent as a word
but before words, before your first
apple there is the brush stroke,
the pen turned around, the ink scratched
through, how rewarding it is to go back and
forth from the physical surface to
its disappearance, in the distance,
outside the frame is the sound of an old milk cart
and because you have not stood still since
there is space, and with it light and shadow
and the subtle gradations of time,
and thankfully for you, and for me,
there is as far as I can see
no discernible vanishing point

Lullaby

Put the sun in your pocket.
Now everything is beautiful like I told you it would be.

Out on the lake the boat is waiting.
The fish are diving. Some of them give their red scales for you

—how kind, how true.

Even the grapes in your hands ripen.

Overhead the moon sails into view.

Walk with me.

Its air is colder. And you are tired.
Touch its light to your lips.
Once more, before sleep can find its way to you.

Breakfast with Yeats

'Even when the poet seems most himself ... he is never the bundle of accident and incoherence that sits down to breakfast; he has been reborn as an idea, something intended, complete.'

W.B. YEATS

Drizzle pouring.

Black hens bespeckling
the place like some insistent mildew.

Everything dotted with them.
Steps, stools, stones.

A tumbly shed, haystacks.
Strutting, calling, and bringing me back to my childhood, to here.

Moment after moment where nothing matters.

Everything from the rain-glistening mountain
to the dog's filthy paw prints on my clean kimono is

exactly the way it is supposed to be.

The Garden

Into the wind, she walks.
The grass gives way before her. Silence is in her hands.

The sky as open as her face. From the water, the birds—

swallows circle her.

Innocence
        —in the speaking house.

And something else.
Call it the shadow. Others have.

Others have said too about its black wings.

The trees bend.
Child, they mean to warn you.

The birch, the cedar.
Do not run from them.

This is your garden, after all. It always was.

And you are home, but do not know it.
You hear the wind and think fire.

You are not wrong.
No matter how much we wish it.

Never

after Maura Soshin O'Halloran

Whale and chrysanthemums
stale on the altar.

I save the wine, chop wood.

There's a novel I want to write.
One thousand days sweeping the floor.

16 grains of rice and two tiny
crawling creatures that didn't need to die.

I lost my voice,
couldn't speak for two days.

After shovelling snow in the sunshine
I felt young again.

Spring thaw:
an old man pushing a black barrow
against the wintry fields.

Coming home in the dusk
the mountains breathe my name.

The Not Told

If I am to believe you,
if I am to believe
you will have me sleeping,
I was not sleeping,
you will have me dreaming,
neither was I that.
If I am to believe you,
you would have the night
pitch and the house
drowned in darkness –
was it ever?
You would have our father
gone, was it ever so?
Our mother fasting,
grieving too.
You would have
the visitation
be a gentle one,
of pulsing light,
of sleek, shrouded figures,
in adopted, religious fervour,
the violence muted.
If there was any, by which I mean,
your protestations—as you have it—
taken then, and replaced
by the gormless, wide-eyed one
who said: 'brother, and son,'
a long time ago—now:
If I am to believe you,
these wilful confessions
are made: after wars,
after births and deaths,
and still I wonder
where you were,
and where you are,
because whoever came back

was not you,
if it ever can have been.
Whenever the switch was made –
for if I am to believe it was,
and I am not to know
who the boy was
who climbed
the wall into the back field,
the one who took
the other by the shirt
and drew blood with his fist,
the one who supped too young,
and was beaten,
where did he go after all?
The secret, the not told,
hovers about your lips,
like flies in summer.
If I am to believe you,
if I am to believe
the flare in the night
is for something else.
The alarm not for us—
but it calls you back—who are you—
to the country we called childhood:
our pale skin is burning
in the sun, our mother
—was it her—
calling out our names
as the light faded quickly.
Listen, if you hold your ear
to this other world,
you can hear the faint echo
of how we once were known:
but the wind is strong,
and it does not want us
to know what you ask me to remember.

Das Internat*   1987

A long train journey
through the Bavarian Alps,
then onto a bus
and into a landscape of snow.

The Internat lay high up
in the clouds. A never
-never land,
where I was welcomed

with a handshake
from the headmaster.
A man who wanted to know
if I liked 'blue movies'.

I didn't understand
the question. I was fifteen.
I went to my room, and
wondered why I was here.

My roommate was Lutz.
He spent his time
with a scissors cutting
the figures of women

out of magazines
and pasting them onto a poster-
board he kept beneath
his bed. I made friends

with the musicians. We
drank beer in the cellar
where we sang songs together.
But soon, the bar was closed.

My German took on
a Southern drawl.
I loved the dialect.
Grüßti.

Weekends were lonely.
One boy crushed aspirin,
mixed it with tobacco
and smoked it. Here, he said

and my brain wavered.
I wrote letters to my girlfriend.
Crazed with teenage longing.
She replied something about braces

for her and a numb tongue.
I ran then too. Miles
and miles across mountain
trails. Next door,

a bearded boy braved
marathons, but wanted to go it
alone. Cut his wrists with a razor
the week before I left.

His girlfriend didn't love him
anymore. The snow
fell, and we drank
a mixture of coke and beer,

in the local cafés,
played pool
and talked long afternoons
away. One weekend

I went home to Frankfurt
with Michael. In a nightclub there,
I drank too much,
was sick outside and left

in the back of a van.
Nearly froze. Days later, I
hitchhiked with Johann.
We were picked up

by a Mercedes.
I cursed in amazement.
Then went to visit his girlfriend.
He emailed

me years later to say
he was living in Lithuania.
Not paradise, he said.
What else? Maths, I couldn't

understand, a weekend
with Lutz and his divorced
mother, who told him to take it
easy when he suggested

he could visit me: when,
when, when? And coming
back to Dublin, to the German
school, to a teacher,

who wondered after
I had servus-ed him, whether
he should have sent me
to the Internat at all,

back to R, and more running,
the Inter Cert,
and the band,
and the memories

of all those boys
who boarded together, sleeping
side by side in the mountains,
how lonely we all were,

with our heads in the clouds;
they, embarrassed by their parents
and far from forgiving them:
how strange to think

of that time now, how
wonderful too, how slight
I was, how unbroken,
carefree and young.

I remember the sensation
of running from a heated pool
into the alpine snow.
It's so long ago now,

but still how precious
it is to recall, to hold the memory
out like a glass of water
and watch it tremble.

*The Boarding School

Heavenly Bodies

Poets have multiplied more than the stars of heaven.
And a poet is an airy thing. Capeesh?
Sleepwalkers, cicadas, and moonlight,
Flying ants, that's more my thing.
And the earth in the distance.
Taxi, taxi—take me there.
And if you talk to the tax man about poetry,
What will you do with the ombudsman
And her smorgasbord?
Tell me, do.
We're going on a hike to the Hellfire Club.
Cards, and a drink with the devil, if you please.
And the trees will end up whispering all your secrets.
Just you see. The only way down is to take flight.
Can you do that? Are you ready?
Take the dead rabbit, its whole body,
as your emissary, if you like.
I don't really care.
Here comes the dusk like a dark music,
Like the sound of a thousand knives sharpening in fact.

Lockdown Haiku-Variations

~1

morning: the magpies screech and rattle
spring sunshine
the island holds its breath

~2

night: a red fox and its cub
saunter down the street unafraid
beneath a super moon's orange light

~3

out walking —
children's toys stare out
the windows of quiet houses

~4

forget the news tonight
I want to hear music
the sounds of something beautiful

~5

I cycle around Marley
its gates are open
but only for cocooners

~6

my mother rings
choc-ices
she wants me to bring choc-ices

~7

on Zoom this morning I talk
with students about Wallace Stevens
about imagination and reality

~8

We're not to feed them bread
The ducks
We're not to feed them peas

But my son still thinks
That they're the best
Because they can swim and fly!

~9

In Marley Park
There is a waterfall
A secret waterfall

My son and daughter run
Over and over the waterfall
They're smiling and laughing

Like nothing has changed
Like everything
Is just as it was

Late Morning Rain—May 2020

the eggs were soft when we went to touch them
it was May, or I imagine it was
though how can I really know it was so long ago
one thing I can be sure of is that summer was on its way
the silent bursting forth which the grass announces
the way it does now on the brink of release
pushing every shadow back to where it belongs
and late morning rain—let's not forget how welcome
that can be, the umbrella forgotten, and all of a sudden
it's forty years ago, and you are walking the same street,
the same road, your hand is in your mother's hand
her face hidden by … what? her fringe, or a hat,
her voice is strong and young, and though she clutches
your fingers in hers, ever tighter now, you do not run
from the shower, you do not rush anywhere

Three Rock Odes

I.

sober light. rain sawing the branches of a tree.
trying to conjure its name.

the teeth of the saw.

indifferent.

the dust of bark. falling. you close your eyes.
stop trying to remember something you never knew the name of.

eyes open. the light. it does not flood anything. it appears.
as it was. ever changing. as it is. constant. like the thing. that is

before us. the thing. we laid to rest. whether we knew its name or
not.

II.

I go there. in dreams.

I relive the moments but without.

I don't say. I don't do. what I did. when I was. without

I profess nothing. and the water is clear. there is.
the pattern in the sand of silver strand and I go there.

without. and everything and everyone is changed.

September

I lay on the floor
with a sack of rice for a pillow
and fell asleep.

In my dream, the monk said to me:
feelings are a distraction,
but you have tried to deny them in the wrong way.

Like walking barefoot on ice.

She said your limits are mostly in your mind.
I was dumbfounded.

Beautiful bald-headed monk, she took me by the hand:

make a ceremony of the everyday,
make a ritual of the mundane.

I woke after three hours.

My mantra was: no distractions, none,

but I failed and planted flowers
for winter instead.

Peonies, fuchsia and narcissus.

Then the rain came.

You were saying

You were saying: how my life was.
We used to run. You were saying: I will start.

Then it's, not at all.

Then one day I won't. I guess.

My older sister. My younger sister. She doesn't trust me.

I suspect.

What else? I suspect. You were saying: I need this tonight.

At least for an hour. Because we're all obsessed with something.
And my dad. My dad has nothing to say to me.

Why don't you tell me about it? You were saying.
I gave up my right to know.

Dublin was beautiful. I found a little cottage with a hole in it.
I need this.

To spend some time together. Line by line.
You were saying: she would hate that.

I would love it. I will start. Everything, everything.
He is there. He can talk. We used to run.

You were saying: I know how to start

You were saying: I gave up my right.
No. No. Not at all.

Night-Shift

my breath reaches his neck —

but the heart is cold
he cannot see me

though he searches
through the streets

in the dark
in the mirrors

all the late sour hours
his custom

by the quays
by the river

over the bridge
driving

this way and that
the metre ticking

over like a countdown
I want to reach out

I want to say something
I want to say—

not sorry
sorry is such a pointless

and stupid word
it can't carry the weight

the range of what I need
to say

to you
daddio

old man
you know how it was

hooked
brooked

bridged
and fucked

the last I know
it was a room

like any other
a score like any other

like all others
did the sun ever

touch me
if you could see me

you would see
through me

it was always thus
autumn in my soul

not your say
daddio

not yours
no

look at all these leaves
in my hands

in my arms
look at you throw

them into the air
and it looks

like laughter
but I can't hear nothing

but the bubble
of speech bursting

like a pocket
of blood

charged with the smack
of all austere

father's
ok daddio

forgive me
for all the light

it floods this cab
like the sun

in winter
for some of us

that's all we need
its gentle bright

twinge
its annihilation

ice cracks
underfoot

walk with me
go on

get out of this black car
I say so

but when I move
nothing

there's nothing
a movement

no
the gesture of movement

I step out of myself
to nowhere

daddio I'm not there
and if you know

I'm not
why then

keep speaking to me
why daddio

keep
telling me

love will save me
when it never did

Nowhere Else

I was on Rathlin trying to write something, a novel, some poems, whatever it was, it ultimately came to nothing; how could it not when it amounted to scraps, pastiche, imitation. It was like so many of our efforts, my efforts—own it—an act of ventriloquism, as if I were playing a role, assuming a voice which did not ultimately belong to me, on an island away from an island, off the north-coast of Northern Ireland in fact, acting out something which was to become, ultimately, my life. It was a place where the puffins came or so I was told, who were, it seems, another set of visitors to intrude upon the peculiarities of this one particular island life— welcome though they were, which could not be said about each and every one of us. Still, there was much to enjoy—though I look back now with bemusement, as I do on so much of my life, as if it had been lived by someone else, a stand-in, or understudy to who I might have been or become. Those weeks were full of incident, more interesting than what my poor imagination suggested to me. The desperation to be recognised as a voice, to be heard, is there anything wrong in that, hampering all the supple and lithe thought which could lead me out of the maze of self-hood. Much to enjoy, much to love, even if it is painful, to go back. I loved, for example, the way the locals did not change their clocks, neither forward nor back, come spring, come autumn, and let time be and do what it did best, which was move inexorably forward with each second: an image of the water high above me: I am clutching the sides of the rigid inflatable boat as it rose and fell against the current's movements. Remember too: the troupe of walkers who arrived one day out of the blue; and with it their laughter, and drinking. Or the divers, I remember them too—their wet suits slung over the harbour railings, the one with the bends holding up the bar, describing his affliction with a loving, if stammering, vivacity, and how they had scoured the MHS Drake, a 14,000 ton cruiser which had been torpedoed by a U-boat in 1917 or the Templemore which sank in heavy weather six years before in Ballycastle Bay and whose boiler section was chock full of conger eels. Or, and less to love than marvel at, there was your man from Belfast who lived on the other side of the island and worked at the Manor house where I was staying, the one who told me my first night that he was not cooking my breakfast, no matter who I thought I was. But I was no one, so he need not have worried. The others, told me he was only *thran*, a word as local as the wily old sheep on the hills, and as rare as the golden hare, or wild orchid of the island, a man who was willing to curse me, for standing up to him, sozzled as he was, and in hiding by the look of it, and wanted by the wrong people. Whatever about him, or the other strangeness of the island: his poor wife who was going away with many wondering whether she would return at all. We were buying our first house then, and not long back from the antipodes, when after staying awake one night in your place on Boyne street, we decided, the newspapers splayed out on the kitchen table, property pages open, to buy a house—ha—with our savings which amounted to zero, but that did not stop us using a credit card, or the courage to place a pin in a map the real estate agent called 'the plans'. What's real about that, or him, I wondered, but fear not—this is all to say, one digression after another, a poetics of sorts after all, that you'll get there one day. But the one thing, I come back to again and again is the girl who came to see the puffins. She looked so lost, as if she did not know what to do with herself, introduced to me on the road lumpy with rocks, a road which would take you, by foot, no fear—there were no cars, around the island back to where you had started, a student of sorts, or traveller, not content with sub-Saharan Africa, or Asia minor. I don't know what her name was, how long she stayed, or where she is now, but she represented something else for me, a figure, lost, arrived too late, and unsure as to her next step, or her next assignment, the way I found myself on the page, a career as anything else lost to me, unsure where to go, circling back on myself, but that there was the house to look forward to, our first home. Remember the green stone I etched our initials onto before placing it into the wet cement as it was being built, a second-self as Jung would have it; it's still there, though we are not. That was before our first child even, all part of a melody I was hearing for the first time, much like the notes of Pergolesi's Stabat Mater traced by my finger and held and guided by yours that one time we had decamped to another house, a rehearsal of sorts, of how to live, of how to be with one another: those notes on the staves—is that what you call them?—like the birds or more specifically the girl on the island, who travelled across the world to see the puffins of Rathlin who were not there. Or like the divers diving for the fresh raw heart of morning. I never knew what it was that made up a poem, I still don't, but that ignorance has served me, it's the ignorance of not knowing what comes next—as if on that stave the quavers, semi-quavers, each musical notation, had yet to be imagined—there was no explanation which I heard for the puffins' absence, no knowing, and even now, somewhere else, someone else, I can still find myself circling the island, in the footsteps of another, listening, be it morning, early so, or late by starlight, or not, even as I walk by the foot of Three Rock, or by Ardglas, Dundrum, and Sandyford, I am there again, with whatever loss, or disappointment the girl felt, I share too, still seeking, still waiting for the notes to arrive, the words to come, like one of those birds, impish puffins, called them tammy noiries, red jimmy's, pelagic, each one, and collectively, an improbability, gathering in the distance, their chainsaw song ringing out, over another sea, another cliff face, somewhere else in other words, where all of us could have happened upon, but for the path we took which has led us to places we would not have anticipated ever coming to, for things which were not there, and brought us, inevitably, it seems, after all, to here, and nowhere else.

Conjugation of an elegy

A house made of matchboxes;
Christmas, I guess. The boxes painted
Mauves, and dull ochres,
And gifts hidden therein—
I do not recall.
A Kindergarten in the 1970s.
A slide, a chase, a scuffed knee.
Memory amazes; is prophetic!
The slide, and chase and blood
Were of things to come.
Imagine it, a lifetime of living
In fairy-tales from another land
In a language which was not your own.

Petrol

It is the right time for dreams.
Through the brick wall, the train.

This stop is secret. East of everything.

Abandoned, disused, where ghosts walk free.

Bully for them.
I wish they would talk to me.

Tell me how it goes. They see but ignore me.
Blame them, don't blame them.

The beautiful delays, and announcements
Are made as if under water.

Where joy once was, there is suffering.
If there ever was any.

Gunshot is audible only to those who have ...
You get the gist.

Flowers, and dreamtime. And where you might have gone.

A death, a bell rung.
More words.
The smell of petrol.
Your dark reflection in its iridescence.

Hospital

A storm. A search.
My hands painting moving hands.

There's nothing there.

Violins
Scrape the walls.
Prayers like aeroplanes—
When lightning hits.

Add it up.
Clap your hands.
Wine like blood.
Then ...

Stillness.
A confession like sunlight.
The end of the storm.

Unter den Linden

The zoo at night.
A child. The croaking lion.

The trees dressed in anger.
Time makes no bargain.
Besides, we've run out of opioids.
The angel drags her feet.
Here come the elephants in the rain.
And the anger in me, like blood in milk.

Nothing civil about this war.

We are the animals roaming the streets.

The German in Me

Make a beach of this border crossing,
Why don't you?
I am so lonely for you,
And the beautiful graffiti you made of my soul.

Meet me at the bridge.
You know the one.
Bring nothing, but the history of the world.
I expect nothing less of you.

You see that clock?
It is a machine of compassionate vengeance.
It is the city's failing heartbeat.
Hurra!

As for the banner you carry,
I'll burn it.
Like I have done so a thousand time before.
Apple scent, almonds, and a shadow

Beneath the machine,
Unnamed.
Cheer again if you like.
You are unburdened.

You are, in fact, delicate like the almond blossom.

Woodsmoke and desire

Can you smell it,
the woodsmoke and desire?

There is a bag full of photographs.
Repose in the past.

And happiness is—
this field on fire.

My world, on the other hand, is covered by snow.

And there is a windowpane you are knocking on:
Let's just say, God is on the other side.

I am a boy again,
on my way to war.

You are too.

Who said this photograph is yours, anyway?

I did.
And God, lest we forget, agreed.

As it is in Heaven

I took these hurts from your eyes.
But they have sprouted.

When I was with you, we travelled
To the other side.

Once upon a time, I was fast.
Now it doesn't matter.

Your curfew is meaningless anyway.
Still, you fled the deserting streets,

Almost naked.

And sunlight lashed you.
Hallelujah!

Dig up the eucalyptus.
You must.

Then watch me cleanse your body, and
Wipe away the scars. Just like that.

If you let me, I can do that.
In the shadows,

Or as you wish.

Go in Fear of Abstractions

Time is baited.
And the forest is alive.
The dry bed of eternity,
where the sun warms nothing
is where you'll find me.

I am afraid to tell you,
I was wrong.
I am afraid to tell you,
You were too.

Why is there a stone in your mouth?

Sometimes, I'd rather live with the animals.
And learn the names of every flower
In this meadow before it is gone.

How can we make that possible?
Do we want to?

From under the grass,
You have no intention of helping.
I know that now.

You hardly have to say it.
Even if the river disagrees.

Call the whole thing

You say gnostic, I say hostage.
I say fear, you say bother.
You say end, I say head.
I say dragon, you say lagoon.
You say rich, I say bitch.
I say gospel, you say hostile.
You say applause, I say please.
I say soul, you say soul.
You say soul, I say soul.

The Secret Life of the Violin

It's after midnight. Ballydehob,
Or Valentia Island.
An Ikea store in China.
A grotto, a cave.
The car abandoned.
The walk steep, but not unwelcome.

Wherever, whatever.
Come with.
Hard hats, and overalls.
Dripping water.
An Olympic year in a slate quarry.

The clouds above are also a part
of the mise-en-scène.
Someone is humming the Stabat Mater.
A Friday of sorrows, and the weather is copacetic.

In the distance are the Skelligs
which we will never make it to
because we are skint.
No matter. It is the dream that counts.

And the violin abides, asleep or meditating,
in one of the fields stitched into your line of vision.
Speaking in tongues again.
Pizzicato. Piece of cake.

Joyless and defeated,
survivors of love gone wrong,
listen to the groove,
and jive of the sacred note.

Be your own light.
Still the monkey mind
with a remembrance of something
from another time.

Something ancient.
And if we need to hitch there,
fear not,
the rapture will be worth it.

Macht Nichts

Lightning,
This time in Weimar,
A balcony. There.

Imagine anything you want for all I care.
Wust. East of nowhere.

(Consider the train tracks.
Or the sunshine to come.)

Or I could say
Shadows make up the past
And what was your life.
Lament it in song.

Please don't. I was only joking.

In the morning after a storm …
Jesus, there was carnage, all manner of
Deceit had gone on, and there was a sing song too.
And a fire if I'm not mistaken.

And Brecht, let's not forget him.

Insects do harm.
I was very sick that summer.
The wind passed through me.
The sun too.

I wrote poems,
Which have been destroyed or lost.
Jealous city,
In your ruins I consecrate their remains.

There is a self
Seeking direction, and a fortune,
If you please.

My soul trod wearily
The road to you know where ...
Tangermünde to Rathenow.

Look it.
I'd do it all again.
I'd do it differently.

Without God.
Without you.

Acknowledgements

Acknowledgements are due to the following publications and broadcasters: *Poetry* (Chicago), *The Irish Times*, *The Stockholm Review of Literature*, *The Honest Ulsterman*, *Looking at the Stars: in aid of the Simon Community*, edited by Kerrie O'Brien, *The Incubator*, *Poetry Ireland Review*. Thanks to Marc Neys for making a film-poem of 'Offering' which appears on *Poetry Film Live* / poetryfilmlive.com, and is part of *The Interpreter's House*, *Sky Light 47*.

The following poems are 'found' poems which sometimes use words, phrases, and sentences from Maura O'Halloran's journal and letters Pure Heart, Enlightened Mind, Riverhead Books, New York, 1994: *Never, Echoes of the One, September, I am a crowd, Love is a Decision*. Thanks too to the editors of The Music of What Happens, New Island, 2020, Breakfast with Yeats, Birdsong, the moon, dlr Local Voices, 2020, the Lyric Note, RTE Radio, The Poetry Archive at UCD, and to the Arts Council of Ireland for a Literature Bursary in 2022.

Cover image "Nouvelle Lune," acrylic, marble powder, and pure pigment on canvas, by Eric Roux-Fontaine, with the artist's kind permission.

PAUL PERRY is the author of five full length collections of poetry including *Gunpowder Valentine: New and Selected Poems*, and two pamphlets of poetry from above /ground press *The Ghosts of Barnacullia*, and *Blindsight*. A recipient of the Patrick and Katherine Kavanagh Fellowship, he is also a novelist. He directs the Creative Writing Programme at University College Dublin.

salmonpoetry

Cliffs of Moher, County Clare, Ireland

"Publishing the finest Irish and international literature."
Michael D. Higgins, President of Ireland